Living Things

LIVING
THINGS

MATT RADER

NIGHTWOOD EDITIONS

Nightwood Editions
www.nightwoodeditions.com

Printed and bound in Canada. This book has been produced on 100% post-consumer recycled, ancient-forest-free paper, processed chlorine-free and printed with vegetable-based dyes.

Nightwood Editions acknowledges financial support from the Government of Canada through the Canada Council for the Arts and the Book Publishing Industry Development Program (BPIDP), and from the Province of British Columbia through the British Columbia Arts Council, for its publishing activities.

THE CANADA COUNCIL | LE CONSEIL DES ARTS
FOR THE ARTS | DU CANADA
SINCE 1957 | DEPUIS 1957

BRITISH
COLUMBIA
ARTS COUNCIL
Supported by the Province of British Columbia

Library and Archives Canada Cataloguing in Publication

Rader, Matt, 1978–
    Living things / Matt Rader.

Poems
ISBN 978-0-88971-223-2

    1. Ecology—Poetry. I. Title.
PS8585.A2825L59 2008   C811'.6   C2008-900040-4

For Melanie & Neela &

Upon an abacus of rain I take a count
Of all living things. I add you and you
And you. My count forever continues

Contents

Notes & Acknowledgements:

Earlier versions of a few poems have appeared or are forthcoming in *Event, Forget, Stylus* (Australia), *The Fiddlehead, Paradigm* (US), *Prism International* and *Memewar*. Thank you to the editors and readers of each of these publications.

"The Ocean Voyager" is a version of Arthur Rimbaud's "The Drunken Boat." It owes a debt to previous versions by Don McGrath and Steven Heighton. *The Ocean Voyager* was fished by John and Ralph Willson. It sank off the west coast of Vancouver Island in 1994. Not long after, John Willson passed. He was followed nine years later by his father, Ralph.

The italics in "Sticky False Asphodel" are from the John Keats poem I know as "There is a joy in footing slow across a silent plain," and from Alexander Pope's *The Odyssey of Homer*.

Living Things was written at Apt. 203, 688 E16th Ave, Vancouver, BC, and at 2250 Patterson St. Apt 85, Eugene, Oregon.

A bead on the abacus for Elizabeth Bachinsky, Treena Chambers, Geri Doran, Elyse Fenton, Karen Ford, Garrett Hongo, Chris Hutchinson, Dorianne Laux, Joseph Millar, Elise Partridge, Michael V. Smith, Russell Thornton, Silas White, Brian Young, and everyone at The University of Oregon for their tutoring on these calculations and many others.

The Great Leap Forward

*

and none and none and none and none and un-

*

zip, a light before light, quickening, like children

*

of early enzymes feasting, each of each, protean
seas gone glacier, gathering footprints, thread, skin

*

for collection at the Exhibit of Humans, a mountain
casting a mould from a city of walls and curs, women
at wash with basins of ashen water and no reflection

*

to recognize their own husbands in a crowded pavilion
of charlatans, quack doctors, snake-oil salesmen
shilling goat glands for impotence, a foolproof gin,
horse semen brandy, and on the buckboard, a Christian
with hurdy-gurdy accompaniment hawking salvation

*

in the antebellum lands, where black winds separate kin
from kin, and the people of the plains hear the coming din
of cattle crossing the continent forty days before it even
begins, and leaded tins of fruits and vegetables poison
Franklin and his men, leaving them delirious and rotten
in the head, composed of thoughts and faith in a northern
passage from ocean to ocean that consumes them like vermin
in the clutch of an owl, picked to pieces, or else frozen

*

in the mind like that line from Keats we failed to learn,
heard melodies are sweet, unheard sweeter, so play on
into the cool afternoon of touching under tables, linen
hung on the line, saxifrage, stonecrop, phlox and gentian,
common-touch-me-not, the meadow beyond our garden
gate opening into bittersweet, death camas, fool's onion,
and again farewell-to-spring arrives in the parched season
of brittle grass, titian leaves, auburn and tawny crimson
infecting the edge of things, as dusk draws from dawn
to envelope us in dark arms like hope or lust, wintergreen,
the flowering weeds we kneel in without naming one
or all or none, for that is a kind of love we call possession
and have abandoned, *Dominus vobiscum*, a woman, a man

Chainsaw

Toothless on Walker's wall, the chainsaw
strung up like any dead animal to bleed out
into a tin a slow viscous drip of black stout.
Walker's workshop was nature's scofflaw,
a backdoor parts-exchange and trophy case
for the age of motorized blades. Saw chains
sagged but held their place in the equation
upon the wall, zeroes like paralyzed faces.
Rosaries of pitch and gauge, Walker prayed
each link with file and rag. When he spoke
the room deepened. Shade bred with shade,
charmed the starter chord, primed the choke.
The motor stuttered and in its stutter talked.
The chain whirled like the hands of a clock.

Domestic Work

You are doing the dishes as you do every night
After dinner and every morning before work
And the light dim over the sink where you sink

Your arms in warm soapy water like a doctor
Elbow-deep in a calving heifer willing to touch
Anything that needs to be cleaned or delivered,

Our silver instruments of custom and manners
Lining the sink like straw in the cowshed stall,
Soiled with saliva and foodstuffs your fingers

Step in as you step in with cloth to clean them,
A soapy mucus greasing the water like blood
On the hindquarters of the heifer and her calf

Who is coming now into the world backwards,
Gangly legs ungraspable in the grasping hands
Of the doctor, sweaty, slick like the silverware

You scrub and slide a washcloth over and over
As if by sheer force and force of will you could
Transform the metal object into a newborn cow,

Woozy in a pool of fluids, wobbly-headed, struck
On its anvil skull by the iron of air and gravity,
And braying like a mule as it teeters underneath

The hull of its mother and braces itself to feed
As all mammals do in the beginning without need
Of knives or forks or fingers but only need itself,

Suds from the cutlery you hold in your hands
Dripping as you run the tap and rinse the tools
And set them upside down in the drying rack.

Compost

in memory of Rodney Mitchell

i.

Chipped enamel of egg, cuttings, kitchen chaff,
coffee grounds ground down to earth by a staff
of earthworms, the compost moulted in its spot
at the garden's verge, a fetid incubator of rot
and flies that let fly when a plank lid was lifted
to slop a bucket of dross and dregs, the graft
and scrap scraped from our picky dinner plates,
the trim and clip of decay off the food we ate.
You maintained it was the place you wanted
to go 'when you go,' to be buried in your own
waste and turned over each spring, to be spread
like manure amongst the flowerbeds and rows
upon rows of vegetables, to grow golden locks
of corn, big-winged rhubarb, sunflower clocks.

ii.

A putrid serving of loamy schlock, a shovelful
of the freshly fashioned dirt was all it took to
birth a bazaar of spring stocks and berserk new
foliage and fruit. A midden of vegetable offal,
each scoop of the shovel unearthed a heat-wash
of insects and enzymes in a teeming underground
of work and work and rework, the silent sound
a red wriggler sings as it excavates our garbage.
But it was the jigsaw of seashells and stone chips
already resident in the earth below the compost
that gave you cause to think we weren't the first
to shuck and dump our foodstuffs at the hip
of that house: the land had long since decanted
the sea where your boots were squarely planted.

To Elyse Fenton's Garden

i.

How does the blue china sky know all about the array
Of blue china plates on Grandmother's dining room wall
As watery portals I dip my finger in to cloud this page,
Or the swifts in the curio cabinet of the chimney stack

ii.

Recall another grandmother's cuckoo clock or my own
Mother's bureau of pewter orioles and school pictures
As reeds in creek mud my water-self breathes through?
With every hollow walnut your walnut eyes meet mine.

iii.

Almost gone under veils of translucent plastic and petals
Of white pear blossoms, blossoms like tiny china cups
And china saucers set out for tea, like a spring snow party,
I can hardly see you now for the care you're swaddled in.

iv.

From sky into sky you raise for me the many coloured flags
Of victory: lettuce, garlic, kale, asparagus, carrot, beets.

From The Lives of North American Trees

Red Cedar

Skinned alive and still I go on into the sky
long after the skinner has expired. I give
of myself freely for you to test and improve
the forms of the forest, to bend and twist my
flesh to your will, to boxes, tools, cordage,
to the masks of your animals who are gone
from this world, while unlike you I remain
resistant to decay, rain, drastic change
of place. This is something you must learn
if you are to survive half as long as I have:
to be flexible, tensile, deeply invested
in real estate. Take a plank from my chest
and fashion of me a home, a ship's stave,
or a cabinet that keeps my scent like an urn.

Sitka Spruce

A Steinway soundboard at core. A knack
for pitch and cords. High strength-to-weight
ratio and knot-free rings mean I sing like
sunlight in honey when played by the right
wind, when let stand in the alluvial pitch,
in the tracks of avalanche, marine terraces,
or wherever else I'm found curing an itch
for the sky. The age of true timber races
by on steel stretchers, borne to the ever after
in a pageantry of dust and gravel, machine
oil, the tuneless cackle of a chainsaw leaping
to life in the woods. A pair of perfect wings
for that garage-built, jerry-rigged aeroplane,
you can almost hear me humming in the rafters.

Douglas Fir

Starter forest. Great for framing-lumber,
wharves once coated in creosote, trestles,
bridge parts. Straight grained and stable,
the timber of choice for slapping together
rafters, joists, the family rancher. I am
the all-American building companion,
light-rosy flesh, favourite of the nation
for Christmas decorations. To God I climb,
on and on into the green storm of my sky,
home to the Bordered White, Engrailed,
and Pine Beauty: Lepidoptera attracted
by the food of my inner light. Sanctuary
from fire for a parish of creatures: slaughter
me and my falling is the Devil's laughter.

A Drawing for Jan Dayman

You are dying and having trouble
So lie in quiet repose with your eyes
Closed as if for practice. I've come
To draw your picture, as if to capture
Your likeness on paper and take it
Away with me would be one less
Thing to slow you on your journey.
I hoke around on the empty page
With my pen until I begin to see
Your earthly features appear there
Pressed into another plane before me
And still, you continue to breathe.

Easter

At Heceta Beach, the tide draws taut
the linen of sand we lay our blanket on
to sleep. But I am a restless sleeper and lie
awake watching the beach roll beneath
the feet of a boy who runs to raise a kite

as the rolling ocean runs to raise the blue
kite of sky above us. In another dream
the ocean too is a restless sleeper who
tosses and turns and curls up in the covers
as I do at home in our bed leaving you

exposed against the cold bedroom wall.
The ravens are fledged shadows aloft,
black flecks on the rolling eye of the sun.
Below the snuffed candle of the light-
house, young arborists scale deadheads

as Christ scaled the cross into heaven
and back again. And when the moon rolls
back the rock of sea tonight, gone will be
any evidence of you or me asleep here,
human on this faithful shore, complete.

Twilight of the Automobile

In the great hall of the woods, a car was stepping down
from its carriage to a fanfare of fir needles and glitter.
The trees stood around vamping in their evening gowns.
My date was missing everything in line for the shitter.
It was all happening too slowly. It was all happening
at a speed too slow to see. We are too late, I thought,
but I was always thinking. Tonight's closed-captioning
was scrolling through the moonlight in an onslaught
of mosquitoes. A bushtit snapped like a photograph
and I was blinded. In the great hall of the woods, a car
was stepping down from its carriage to the paparazzi
of rust and twigs. The trees were begging for autographs
and tossing their hair. My date came back with a star
in her pants and she took off her clothes to show me.

Common Carrier

i.

Together, together, together, tethered
container to container, a caterpillar
with no chrysalis except to get there
and unload the cargo. I go forward.

ii.

I go backward. I go where the tracks go
and I go slow. I'm old but not as old
as coal or steam or hydro. When it's cold,
the switching yard crystalled in snow,

iii.

I still tow the fields of harvest wheat
from prairie to coast, the vast ocean
of ethanol a slosh in my middle hold.

iv.

Trained to trains crossing city streets,
I'm stolen away in my sleep. Behold
that lumbering locomotive, emotion.

National Research Council Time Signal

Ten seconds of silence—God has gone
        back into the laboratory: the ash outside
            the office window is at work on new heraldry

            and the Clippers have a three-games-to-one lead
        in a best-of-seven series. A cure for cancer
has been chewed in the gum of the yew,

but few will ever taste it. Eight hundred
        gallons of water is all it takes to make one
            hamburger and that shirt sloganeering *Green*

            on Main Street holds twenty-five bathtubs
        in its molecular history. Chances are we've
taken a bite of each other, literally, at some

point in our lives. Great codes are sojourning
        in our DNA, to paraphrase a young doctor
            I read the other day. Even birds understand

            grammar. Which is to say, we are not alone
        any longer. Everything is larger. The sun
won concessions from the stratosphere,

meaning a cabal of hydrocarbons and UV
     lighting now controls the picture. Easier
          to engineer a new face than look yourself

          in the mirror. Cryptozoology or the Ark-
     of-the-Disappeared: it appears the average
London cabbie has a pumped hippocampus

on par with those creatures who use sonar
     to navigate troubled waters. I'm sure you've
          heard the saying recently, *bombing for peace*

          is like fucking for war, but research revealed it
     to be true in the cloning of stars. This has been
a test. *The beginning of the long dash—*

You, Louis MacNeice

My face in the train window
Glows black and cold.
I look but do not recognize
Eyes worn blank and old
While over the wold
The train unspools its shadow.

The last epoch of vast travels
Unravels and knots;
I am headed home by steel thread,
Dead to every thought
As the train dreadnaught
Fires nonstop its piston gavels.

The hills are gone to gorse fires.
Gross spires of smoke
Needle the sky into a pall
All suffer and choke
As all things are yoked
By the lion hurt of Earth's desires.

Then gathering its shadow
Slow from the fields
The train returns my world weight,
Waits and waits and yields:
A second train revealed
And faces in the black windows.

Wildfire

Burst forth from the mountains in search
of what remnants of forest it had not scorched,

what trees cowered in the shapes and structures
of the city, disguised and harboured by new strictures

of function and utility. Parasite or curse, a war
like virus, descendant of what smoked the star

fish on the coast, smallpox, rubella, tuberculosis,
the Catholic host, all that communion or symbiosis

between agents of infection and the subconscious.
We burned every form of wood—conscience

be damned—that surrounded the town in hopes
it would slow the thing down, a scorched rope

of land where no fuel could be found. The sun set
and a new sun played on in place of the forest.

From The Lives of North American Trees

Red Alder

A hotshot. Among the first into disturbed
lands. I blaze red under this smoker's skin
and lichens—we hip have our hangers-on—
and pedal nitrogen to the earth like words
to the poet's pen. Fuck him for dodging me
this long. I'm common. Snort my pollen
in spring and you'll know who I am. When
you're stuffed and swollen, I'll be randy
as a bull moose in the mood, all my lungs
sawtoothed and coarse and sucking back
your second-hand breath like I've nothing
better to do, my cones and catkins trolling
for wind-tricks on riverbanks, slide track,
the floodplain where we abandon our young.

Broadleaf Maple

An armoire, rocking chair, baby grand—
When will you play me a melody, hold me
in your arms, secrete my unmentionables
in the cavity of your heart? Tell me. All
winter I go skin and bones in the insufferable
cold and never once do you come to stand
beneath my splayed and naked body
to offer protection or even the biting scrawl
of your confessions. I will tell you this:
come the stop-motion explosion of spring
I will scatter volunteers across your garden,
an army equipped to march into the ring
of your command, to shoot like men
into the earth. That my friend is a promise.

Bitter Cherry

I'm smooth as old scar tissue, a familiar
excuse, calloused hands on a hickory haft.
Collared, chaste, I rise in back draughts
of sin and corruption, the cheap bazaar
chainsaws and weather, God's ill-temper,
render the world. A pious loner, no grove
of my kind will ever be found: we love
no one but ourselves and need no other
but wind to wind the clock of our issue.
Stone-hearted stigmata, my fruit weeps
from blossoms of blushing white, vellum
I ash like cigarettes. A dark, bluish hue
in the bark says I'm old blood. Lo, reap
my acrid yield and taste of His kingdom.

The Age of Snow and Wood

When we were young the woods lay down for us
our dark fuel. And grown we took their cores
for violins, aeroplanes, heated homes. Tonight, the snow
wanders like men from the dark woods of the sky
to fence posts and car hoods. And the mills of the coast
roll out acre after acre of white paper. Our fathers'
lungs are black forests where a lost soldier wanders
like snow into the blood. And from the stand of smoke-
towers on the horizon, this century's coiling umbilici
to the last and first fire. Snowflakes flirt in captions
of light above the sidewalk and children lay down
their likenesses in the mounting dust. When we were
young the dark woods of the sky lay down for us
white reams over a copse of homes and chimneys.

Mustang

No more racehorse. We showed her no mercy:
Stoned out of our stupid ever loving minds,
Half-cut, underage, ready to tempt any kind
Of line we came across, and yet somehow we
Always made it home safe, my brothers and me
(No jail or pregnancy and only one bloody nose

To speak of but don't). Who bloody well knows
How close we came to the edge, what mercy
Moved those telephone poles buried as landmines
At the side of road, or smothered the sirens we
Heard in the distance trailing us wunderkinder
Of luck by seconds not minutes. My girl and me

Liked to park and fuck or she'd just take me
In her mouth as I drove the coast trying to nose
The needle and us into the unknown. My kind
Of ride. My kind of horse. Please, pay no mind
To the rubber we left behind like a worm of mercy
On the asphalt, a gesture to the old gods we

Aimed to replace. Wherever we wanted to go we
Went in her leather interior, my brothers and me,
Drinking Lucky Lager and rolling doobies. Mercy
On those who got in our way. I had it in my mind
She'd never die. Then, oozing like a child's nose,
The engine spread a quilt of green and kind-

Red colours in the carport. We weren't the kind
To monkey with motors or carburetors or wee
Cracks in whatever-the-hell-it-was deep in the mind
Of that machine that drooled its unwanted mercy
All over the place. We kept driving, our noses
To the grindstone of our own demise, the shimmy

Of the engine into ever higher registers a meme
We'd all been infected by so ignored as any kind
Of sign. When a horse falters, no time or mercy
Will make her show any better. *Wowee Zowee*
Was still ten years out of reissue and our minds
Soaked in its weird from the stereo. No one knows

Just where we go when we go. Some folks diagnose
Jesus, Jell-O, scrap metal; give me a mercy of mind
Of the kind that Mustang gave my brothers and me.

The Weather Makers

We carry it with us wherever
we go, like germs or secrets,
genetic predispositions

to illness. It dogs us, has our scent,
our number, an uncanny knack
bordering on the psychic to know

where we'll turn up next and be hot
on our heels or already there
waiting to greet us. A crooked wire

of lightning we snagged
in the undercarriage and dragged
across the badlands, that long scratch pad

of highway to come-what-may and everything
after. Unshakeable, we wake to hear it
stomping on rooftops, tapping

like small rocks against the window
of our hearts, or knocking out
the power like artillery in some Iraqi

province. Socked in and stalked by
cloud cover sent in the spirit of good
detective work or bounty hunters

meant to bring us to justice,
we are on the lam from our own
Captain Ahab, Pat Garrett, guilt

over those early experiments
in greed and curiosity we could say
created the situation at hand. Next time

we are in your town, watch for a twister
to touch down a few inches from where you stand.
All it takes is a whiff. Tag. You're it.

The Birds of Canada

I am driving a freeway in another country
When on the shoulder a blown tire becomes
A carcass for two turkey vultures turning
As on a child's mobile above this crib
Of continent and I remember the shoji
Screen in your apartment, silk-screened
With two green herons and your silhouetted
Body. You undressed in troubled modesty
Behind the herons' geisha fan of wings
While my mind circled your body being
Shaped and unshaped behind the screen.
And all at once all the birds of Canada,
Bushtits and juncos and sparrow hawks
Red-winged blackbirds, blue jays and harriers,
More birds than I could name including
The great blue heron, sandpiper and vireo,
Turnstone, merganser, mourning dove,
Skylark, the lesser scaup, the oldsquaw,
Ravens and crows, even the last great auk,
Lift into the sky, an enormous shoji screen
Of feathers and wings and the sun a shoji lamp
In the early hours of the twenty-first century.

Fastest Man on the Planet

Citius, altius, fortius

Over before you know it. A curve
    in the space-time continuum and so
        quick he's looking himself in the back
           of the head just as the race is about to
               begin. He's already won, or will win,
           once the race is run, but from the couch
        at home, where we've just recently tuned in,
      the announcer is cautioning us not to rush
to judgment on this one. Anything can
    happen between now and then, he says,
        which is where our runner is at this very
           instant, vanished from our TV set, like
              so much of our lives given over to watching
           this dreck. Hard to believe we'd take
        the bet given the odds things would turn out
    different from the way they will or did, but
who's kidding who, we've covered the spread
    and are ready to kick back and crack a beer,

    the fastest man on the planet was just here.

High Noon

Since the stereo's digital display
         Flashes twelve o'clock—
Noon or midnight, all day—
And darkness keeps furtive glances under lock
         And key, we play
         The movie and the part, don't talk,

         Just watch our man Cooper silently sink
         Like his shadow,
Into the pale, dusty sink
Of midday sun, angle, his own ego,
         Shrinking in sync
         With what we think and think we know

         Of those we committed ourselves to
         Through marriage
Or profession, the true
Value of your companions and courage
         When fate tags you
         And you go alone into carnage—

         There is no such thing now as a fair fight.
         Even the sun
Has no power, no might
As arbiter of time. We mark high noon,
         Midnight, by sleight-
         Of-hand, electronics, the train

Schedule in the film where the train arrives
For once, on time,
That moment in our lives
When to run from someone becomes a crime—
Our Lord forgives.
Grace Kelly shoots a lone hoodlum

In the back, kills him. Cooper kills the rest.
I feel your knee
Against mine. The old west
Loved outlaws, gunslingers. I love the steady
Nerve we divest
Of with our clothes, our enemies.

Iceman

Dig him in his element: the coolest man
on the planet. Centuries ahead of us

in death and dying: cryogenically composed,
freeze-dried with classic, copper-age tech

perfect for forensics to cast their magic on:
a test of isotopic composition, gut content,

carbon-dating, has natural causes, accident,
sheer bad luck hard-boiled to a sinister plot

of unknown origin. Confirmed is the presence
of another man's blood on his knife and yet

another man's on his cloak. A shoulder wound
in the shape of an arrow matches what we imagine

the shape of an arrow wound to be. Evidence
suggests a hankering for chamois and deer

and a handful of blackthorn sloes in lieu
of beer or wine before that final ascent

into the mountains. Charted, drawn, inked in,
fifty-seven tattoos says Fritz was a colourful

specimen, but we all know it's the shoes
that make the man, and his were bearskin,

waterproof and wide, designed for walking
on snow. To follow in his footsteps

is where the young and hip can expect to go.

The Ocean Voyager
In memory of John and Ralph Willson

Comes the wayward waters of the coast
Bearing me on its unbroken back, chartless,
Without compass or sextant, no ghost
Or unseen hand guiding me by cutlass

Or caress: I enter Hecate the only captain
This vessel will ever know—To hell
With illness-stitched wool, English pain
Balled in musket shot, delicate otter shells

Piled like money in the hold, I sold
The treacherous lot to the sea, the boatmen
Tagged and taken by whitecaps, lassoed
To the beach, wrecked and erected as totems

By panther-eyed armies of salal and skin,
Omens for the coming centuries painted
The ever green of cedar and greed. No sin
Shone from a lantern's idiot eye; no tainted

Light spewed from the moon, splattering
In the Pacific mist like insects. Darkness kissed
The phosphorescent salmon chattering
At my hull and scrubbed the stains of piss

And wine and filthy commerce from my deck.
Emptier than a child's mind, I made
The scrambled brains of Desolation on-spec
My thirteenth day where the tidal braid

Of the strait cradled and rocked me to sleep
Like your whiskey. A pale bag of deer
Bobbed at my ribs, uncorked from the deep
Well of the lived. I danced troughs like fear

On nervous highways, two-stepped crests
Like early love, and since then I have flown
Lightning wracked seas in the fissured west,
Known what men thought they've known.

The low sun slouching steadily towards Japan
Dragging white contrails across the screen
Of the atmosphere, the sea's eyelids frozen
Shut by shards of stars, the maddened screed

Of waves like buffalo stampeding to oblivion
Upon the shore. I have dreamed the curdled
Hand of ice in harbour, for the nattering wind
A muzzle, crows hauling dawn across the world.

To be sure, I've hunted Haida Gwaii like
A hound, nosed its monkey beach with my keel
Then turned on the wheel of the ocean, flocks
Of glaucous in the endless seas above reeling

With me, southward through the kelp-nets
And fermenting weeds, the forever drizzle
Like chains hanging from heaven's basement.
Orca offal in the tidal flats, the mud's missal

Of decay and puzzle, a rotting hull of ribcage.
I note these things along the way, a hoard
To lord over and over, arrange and rearrange
Upon the galley-bench of mind searching for

Order. Glinting teeth of glaciers cut seawards
Over thousands of years but I will not rudder
Or tack here and no creature nor any words
Alive today will be so when these beasts shudder

And make their move to water. I would
Show children those oolichan like candles
Burning beneath the surface, the driftwood
Castles yet to be imagined on the beach, mantles

Of foam and salt the drowned will shoulder
Like boas from a rubber tree. On my gunnels
Dance shore birds the weight of a lust-whisper
In the ear. Comes running through runnels

Of air, the landfall gossip: floating islands
Like glass fishing globes snatched from the map
For souvenirs. Water-drunk, sea-canned
By briny slosh, my staves won't rot or snap

And release me finally to the silent squelch
Of the depths, fathoms beneath in the birdless
Pitch where I would remain like a ship's wench
On her knees, gladly, to be relieved of the aegis

Of my own fate, saved from the sobbing breast
I have suckled too long now with its shadow
Flowers and jelly-wasps; no old galleon guest
On this coast nor armoured monitor would know

To dredge the surface for my prow; riddled
With lichens of pale sun, barnacle-tumours,
Azure phlegm, I drift of my own unbridled
Arrogance never coming up against the rumoured

Wall of the sky reddened by the savage blood
Of pilgrims beating their heads out of this
Labyrinth-mine. I've weathered tsunami and flood,
Maelstroms of fifty twisted leagues, behemoths

Of wind hammering nights sidereal architecture
Its scuddering floes of cloud skewered on
Mountain parapets, the firmament fractured
And opened to swallow sailors and all gone

Wanderers save me. Is it in such elemental
Rapture that you exist, exiled with the golden
Plover, the lapwing, caught in the career and pull
Of here to there and never anywhere you happen

To be, simply, at the moment? I fear the acrid
Torpor of this love. I desire a black pond
Of frogspawn, a sad child burdened by limpid
Eyes folding an origami boat to chart reed fronds,

Or a mayfly cocooned in paper and set free
By fingers from the prison-ship of its first form.
Such forlorn languor as I call home, I do not see
History's electric Diogenes pass over me in alarm.

Emergency Broadcast System

When the radio cuts out in a fit of static
or the picture goes blue for half a sec-
ond longer than I'd expect or the lights flick
off in perfect weather, I'm always quick

to think, *This is it*, the one we've all been
waiting for, the news we knew to imagine
but could not imagine nonetheless, the end
of life as we live it, careless in this land,

and when you let go of my hand and stand,
balanced by your own mass and muscle,
a fresh knack for gravity at your command,

begin to look around, wonder, slyly smile,
then, one foot in front of the other, totter
forward into the future, fearless, my daughter.

Aeons

Leaves are swooning in the streets. Kids tear up
alleyways in toe-worn kicks for one last glimpse
of the brickwork corner store before the bulldozer
does her in. Road Works calls it quits mid-business
citing winter weather, water table, uncertain soil

conditions. One shift of tectonics and the Pacific
shelf is in the kitchen. The Imperial Soviet Museum
draws black behind the wings of a teratorn skeleton
spirited from the Siberian icefields. Word is tiny
people may still exist on this Earth and Irish elk

are not Irish at all. Headlights on bedroom walls
are comets clearing the solar system or just folks
heading home for one last go at dinner with the kids,
that something to someone left unsaid. My love,
it all comes flooding back epoch by epoch, the dark

nights of the ice age, those early caves, mastodon
and mammoth of the Great Plains, primeval seas,
Pangaea, the Big Bang. We are travelling through
creation in a blink, age after age, pages in a heavy
unwritten volume on the history of men and women.

From The Impostor's Guide
to North American Plants

False Solomon's Seal

In the great grimoire of grifters, gamblers and good-
For-nothings she gets no love. Her forged signets
Summon no jinni or demon or royal lineage. A rood
Of leaves screens a chancel of flowers and garnets
From her dark stalk but few believe she's any more
Than a tiny galaxy of white stars and bitter planets
Unspoken for by nomenclature or magic. An actor,
Find her spikenard-scented in lowland meadows,
A doily of flowers flaunted like the feathered oar
Of a junco mid-stroke, or purled in fens and fallows
Her fleshy stout rhizomes persistent as personhood
Among all peoples. Go now. Name your shadows.

False Lily-of-the-Valley

Broad-hearted and hardy, what mother wept you
In the New World as Mary wept the Golgotha dust
Into lilies-of-the-field? Christ's farewell, adieu,
Sign-off sermon never mentions you. If Zeus, lust-
Struck, screwed Maia good and gave her Hermes
Then who gave you *maianthemum dilatatum*? Trust
The taxonomists to dig Maya Angelou. Japanese
Sounds you out as "Russian Mouse," but I'd go
Hardcore like Dragonslaughterwort. I josh. I tease.
St. Lenny of the Viennese spoke Austrian, ergo,
I don't know what the fuck he'd call you. So who
Are you? Rogue? Hero? Lookalike-slash-alter-ego?

Fool's Onion

Starflower? Grass Nut? Pretty Face? Let us cure you
Of your pride and misconceptions: we're no tonic
For your baldness or plague panacea. Here's a clue:
We go by many aliases gifted from you. Ironic?
Define irony. I dare you. Peel us and reveal what
Exactly? Stalks of pink and purple-blue? Laconic,
Sardonic, but true. You've likely seen us in low-cut
Grasslands, mountain meadows, a tortured sward
You trampled through. But your big brain was shut
To the names of things like us, so pushed forward
Without further issue. Wild hyacinth. That's us, too.
You know the score, you're disguised as the Lord.

False Pixie's Cup

They're them. Not quite the complex Eisenhower
Warned us of it's true, but close enough. Say
What you will, a million bucks says when our
Number's up these guests of Precambrian decay
And humus will lift their tiny ghoulish goblets
Into the haze, among the lingerers in life's soiree
With cockroaches and poetry. Came up doublets
They did so who knows which from which. Faction
Not fashion makes all the difference. Now let's
Imagine ourselves as a set, each of us a fraction
Of an indivisible whole, sepals on a giant sunflower.
We all turn from cloak to clock. We take action.

Sticky False Asphodel

The last meal the ghosts of unimportant people
For all eternity eat in Homer's bog meadow
Is the ashen bog-asphodel. Gods and laypeople,
The Elysian Fields and the untrodden meadow
Of asphodel Louis MacNeice imagined a foot
Poised over, the other to the ankle in a meadow
Of Irish peat and sticky asphodel. *O to foot*
Slow o'er ever-flow'ring meads of false asphodel
And Dutch daffodils. By mile, chain, yard, foot,
The dead collect like we chanterelle asphodel
For soups and salads. In the beds of many people
Grow small deaths. Outside, sticky false asphodel.

On First Looking into Larkin's "Aubade"

I get up each day in the dark and in the dark go
To sleep half-drunk, having said not half what
I meant to say to those I love or love to know
Only by sight: the gypsy-eyed girl and the mutt
Outside the market where I buy coffee and bread
Each morning and toss a few coins in her cup;
The Korean dude next door I've given up
Talking to, to whom I give only a nod of the head

And who gives up nothing of himself in return.
I stand in the carport at half-four and smoke,
The world soft around the edges, soon to relearn
The shape light brings to juniper and oak,
How what we see in daylight is less than whole
And also more so, how we distinguish things
From things in a catalogue of being
We call the complete picture: what wicked toll

We pay for the sleep we receive after dusk:
Each dry hour upon hour of work and solitude
In our own inescapable skin. If death is the musk
Men like us smell and awake to, that exudes
From every living thing the moment we are
Exhumed from the dark to that last birth back
Into oblivion, it's fear of love that attacks
Our sleep and leads us alive from library to bar

To books to bed without speaking. Such shade
Leaches sweetness from living. Light after light
Winks awake on my street, and I am made
And unmade by the nagging thought of what might
And might not be. No god serves also those
Who stand and wait for no god serves anything
Save itself. I am at odds with my own thinking
And the ghosts I wear on my mind like clothes:

The sweater the gypsy girl filched from my truck
When the weather turned. I smile and swear
Every time I see her shivering with bad luck,
Tucked into her Shepherd mutt, that ugly sweater
I used to wear wearing her there in the wet cold,
As just now, the Korean dude on his back stairs
Steps down into the half-dark, half-lit, unaware
I see him adorned in dawn's thin garment of gold.

Firewood

i. The Woodpile

Wind-cured through a rift in the weather,
the woodpile waits to be puzzled back
together, riddled into what we remember
of last year: neat walls of heft and stack
beneath the sun-deck, paid on their own
weight by careful hands wary of collapse,
buttressed with a crisscrossed column
at each end, yet easy access for the axe.

Four cords to split and bank for winter
no crude architecture could reassemble
the way the wood would by very nature:
at crux and core of our fuel-hoard, a vole
whelp wiggles blindly, a verdant guest
and harvest of the once and future forest.

ii. The Woodstove

The heavy cast-iron heart of the family
room. Ash-vault. Coal-urn. Manifold fire
box with air wash and baffle. Our old Fire
King, all heat-waffle and carbon-kitty,
holds forth on its tiled hearth as I work
to bank the morning fire: a circus tent
of newspaper and kindling and turbulent
flame that bursts the wood like a cork.

And warmed, the house-pulse quickens
as water vapour and gas flash in the flue
and the smoke-light collapses to ember
as sleepers awake as sleep unthickens
the wood-grain releases the wasp anew
and singed, out slithers the salamander.

Deer
For Russell Thornton

Trip a switch somewhere and there he is
like flame on a matchstick or a coin
tricked from behind the ear: a deer,
or the ideogram for a deer, blazing
in the lowlight of your evening garden,
a vision foreboding the end of your roses
or something colder, a backhanded compliment
on your efforts to rope wilderness, the fence
of freeway that keeps predators
in check around the village, your own hunger
to encounter the edge of another
dimension and be stopped in your tracks,
caught staring at a creature who materialized
before your very eyes and now stares back.

Alligators

Elsewhere, the levees breached, the alligator
scuttles and snaps like wire in the low water
street. Witness oblivion in that unhinged maw:
the cameraman's calf in the thresh of the jaw,
tendons ribboned with ragged hiss and gnash.
Crowds cinch and cringe each twitch or thrash,
while waylaid, our gator is all feint then scurry,
circling and circling in the blood and slurry.

Change channels. Long in Lower Yangtze
River, fenland vaults possess orient treasure:
the mythic pike-head lizard at weathered ease
in mud-heat of decaying leaves. What measure
of epoch does the dragon take? What winter
will wink out with no word of the alligator?

Frogs

Little hobgoblins of muck, coagulated mud,
they come back to me each spring like rust
on the underbelly of a newly painted truck,
like wobbly pox (throbbing drumskins of guck

unstuck from their winter hovels in the flesh
of the creek bed) like a thrombosis of fear, like thrush
in the hoof of the ear. Marshalled in the marsh-
lands, they drag me nightly by the mind-rushes

into the reeds, thrash me with sedge and leave
me for a moment, mugged of myself, relieved.

The Great Mink

Makes eyes from his mud-blind
in the riverbank as we await,
water-locked to the waist,
courage to submerge
in the flex and tug
of the current. Wink back
and his whole body blinks,
skitters and shrinks
down the throat of his escape hatch,
then slinks back, turtles
to the tunnel mouth all coy and quietly coquette.
Purse perfect and plush, flush
with a false confidence,
our water-weasel wheels rock
to rock in a hurricane of reconnaissance
before pouring his entire contents
—hat-fur, chisel teeth, skin-bag of ancient remedies—
riverward and harrying shore to shore,
a harbinger with a world to warn.

From The Lives of North American Trees

Western Hemlock

Kept in the dark, cast in the deep shadow
of cedar and fir. A squirt. A spindly
secret at work in the underbrush, quietly
vying for a place in the canopy. Slow
and shallow my root system octopuses
through the raw humus of a nurse log
as I lift myself above the Pacific bog
of the forest floor and continue upwards
like the flag of the conqueror rising over
Baghdad or Rome. I am the climax
species, the bringer of a new order to
this empire of trees. I will use my power
to set things right, shower shade on those who
held tight to the sun until the very last.

Garry Oak

Warped, twisted, bent out of shape, cured I con-
form to no straight plane. Good for nothing.
Knock-kneed, knobby, in need of a cane,
I'm age encased in scaly skin, catkins dangling
like pendulums set to keep a kind of time
continuing, tear-shaped acorns built to bomb
blue camas, fescue, the grass-toothed combs
and gall wasps, the glacial outwash I call home.
Always a flush of clubs in my hand, no bluff.
The cards are dealt and to the winner the land
to erect a stand of houses as he sees fit, a cask
of flesh for wine. All the thunder god asks
is no forgiveness for the swine that made the man
who would go all in for anything less than life.

Arbutus

Heart on the sleeve. Bad skin. Like you,
I'm twisted, kinked, all knotted up inside
with shame and embarrassment: to survive
when so many have perished around you,
cut down in their prime for the lesser crime
of being strong and straight and available
on a mass scale. Windfirm. Hardscrabble.
I unravel a standard in the rock and grime
of the subsoil, where you too will return
in the postburn of your life. Regenerative
through fire, through blowdown, a globe-
shaped burl sleeps furled in the earth, alive
with the codes of these blushing robes,
so unlike you, I'm sure: I die to be reborn.

War

When no breath issued from the big house but their own
And all the slavers were slaughtered in the aster and lupines,
And the tide paused like a knife at the throat of the dyke,
I imagine the Comox, haggard and pollocked with guts,
Going corpse to corpse like priests in chasubles of muck
To anoint the skulls and preserve their enemies' deaths
With a club, the dirt and hassocks outside the house soggy
With blood and warm between the toes (one man no doubt
Thought of his woman's mouth), each man takes in his
Hands the hands of his butchered kin or his kin-in-war
And drags them like sleds of flesh across the campyard
To the shore where sweat-matted dogs arise like smoke
From hiding holes to growl and yap for scraps, the cock
And balls and scalps the Comox shuck and toss on the rocks
Like fish heads for gulls, the eagles in the cedar trees
Like banquet guests before the feast, jawing over the dish
Of entrails the dogs have made of the beach, and because
It is all dispatched from my mind's eye anyhow, I dispatch
A flotilla of Comox to paddle the estuary in the glistening
Noonday sun and climb, through the dark sentinels of fir
And hemlock, through meadows of purslane and starwort,
The far hills of the valley to the plateau that overlooks
The estuary and the big house and the fields of killing,
Which are also fields of ducks and swans and flax flower,
Breathless through burnet and sweetgrass and strawberry
And a fit of whisky jacks, to where the women and children
Of Comox took refuge that day and like daylight vanished.

Visits to the Royal
British Columbia Museum

Here is the Garden of Eden.

Here are the women
That work in the Garden of Eden.

Here are the baskets
Woven by the women
That work in the Garden of Eden

Here are wool blankets
Piled in the baskets
Woven by the women
That work in the Garden of Eden

Here are the muskets
That enforce the blankets
Piled in the baskets
Filled by the women
That work in the Garden of Eden.

Here is the ship of Captain Vancouver
That conjures the muskets
That enforce the blankets
Piled in the baskets
Carried by the women
That work in the Garden of Eden.

Here are cedar and spruce, grizzly and cougar
Seen from the ship of Captain Vancouver
That delivers the muskets
That demand the blankets
Piled in the baskets
Conscripted by the women
That work in the Garden of Eden.

Here is a man in a black raven mask
Of cedar and spruce, grizzly and cougar
Seen from the ship of Captain Vancouver
That summons the muskets
That secure the blankets
Piled in the baskets
Shouldered by the women
That work in the Garden of Eden.

Here is the world in an old tin cask
Given the man in the black raven mask
Of cedar and spruce, grizzly and cougar
Seen from the ship of Captain Vancouver
That supplies the muskets
That sweeten the blankets
Piled in the baskets
Indulged by the women
That work in the Garden of Eden.

Here is a girl that taps the glass
To test the world of an old tin cask
Traded the man in the black raven mask
Of cedar and spruce, grizzly and cougar
Seen from the ship of Captain Vancouver
That supplies the muskets
That infect the blankets
Piled in the baskets
Carried by the women
That work in the Garden of Eden.

Now are the days and the school and the class
That teaches the girl that taps the glass
To test the world of an old tin cask
Traded the man in the black raven mask
Of cedar and spruce, grizzly and cougar
Seen from the ship of Captain Vancouver
That return the muskets
That rejoin the blankets
Piled in the baskets
Abandoned by the women
That work in the Garden of Eden.

This is your neighbour home from Mass.
Now are the days and the school and the class
That teaches the girl that taps the glass
To test the world of an old tin cask
Shown the man in the black raven mask
Of cedar and spruce, grizzly and cougar
Seen from the ship of Captain Vancouver
That carries the muskets
That explain the blankets
Piled in the baskets
Displayed by the women
That work in the Garden of Eden.

The Worm Compost
for Melanie

Tonight, in the black box of our storage closet,
a black box of plastic records our eating habits
in a soggy thresh of newsprint, an exquisite text
of worms and leaves and pH balance you upset
once every couple of months to parse our future
through clues in the muck: cairns of sheep shit
or entrails in a soothsayer's dish, you predict
a parliament of annelids to get us back to nature.

Proof

Breath plumes with every down swoop of the axe,
my warm-bloodedness tested and attested to
by the cold white plumage—I pause
amongst the holocaust of kindling
to watch you through the kitchen window,
at work on your own proof with milk and sugar,
a splash of flour in your hair revealing a *you*
still sometime in the future—when out of nowhere
the air dapples with Christmas carols,

                                    and a helicopter
crests the rooftops, a looming airship,
wobbly at first in the white incense of wood
smoke coiled above each house,
and then, as if ratified and blessed, blowing clear
overhead bearing gifts: airmen, music.

Pietà

Put an ear to the wall of air arisen around you
and tell me what you hear: *You cannot stay here*
Forever. Wrapped in an afghan of silver frost,
The winter trees lower the sky onto their shoulders.
Shimmy the old oak and press your face into heaven.

Reading with Neela

In my office, behind cairns of books and papers,
Your too-young-to read reading voice visits me
From a room down the hall where you've found
A rocking chair to set rocking and a storybook
To prompt your own story. Eager to hear it all
I open a book of poems to where a poet's crock
Of snow water awaits my kettle, and select from
My library the most delectable infusion of pages
To brew for tea. In the reading room of my ear
I serve your voice a tray of finest china and Oregon
Honey and a tea I call Many Years of Reading.